Terrified

Terrified

Pick up this book if you're scared or in trouble

Sabre Gustaf

Published by Tablo

TABLE OF CONTENTS

ABOUT

THE BOOK

There is a lot of crazy stuff happening in the world and you can get into deep trouble seriously quickly. If this ever happens to you then the information in this book could help you to get through that time safely. This is the book I wish someone had written for me and I wrote it for myself. I've decided to share it with the world so if anyone is scared or in trouble then they can easily access this information too.

THE AUTHOR

I have got myself into some strange and dangerous situations. I've been through the military, have worked in crisis management teams for global companies, have taken part in extreme sports and have done lots of other things. Along the way I've seen people I care about hurt themselves, get admitted to psych wards, go bankrupt, wind up in jail, complete good work for destructive organisations, cause pain to other people, become trapped in cults and die. I know how quickly things can go wrong and I know what it takes to work through complex situations while terrified.

THE START

Anxiety can be a powerful indicator that something in your life requires attention. A proper dose of anxiety can feel almost unbearable and, in response to that feeling, you may go looking for ways to escape your reality, change your circumstances, deny your situation or fix yourself. During that time you can make some stupid decisions and you may also be vulnerable to anyone who can sell you an answer to your perceived or actual problem - even if what they are selling isn't true or good for you.

In this world there are perfectly legal and completely illegal traps, often presented as opportunities, that aren't designed for your benefit. Instead, they are tailored for you in order to produce results for other people. To avoid, navigate and escape these traps safely there are some basic concepts about life that are really important to know. I have spent several years summarising these concepts into the following short chapters which can be read in any order.

ILLUSIONS OF CONTROL

Right now there is more happening than our minds can compute. Billions of people are going about their lives and at each moment our bodies are regulating themselves while engaging with a broader ecosystem that sustains life itself. The earth spins, stars explode, children are born and a person who wakes up in the morning is different to the person went to sleep at night. They have literally moved through space and time so it's funny to hear people say things like "you've changed" as though it's a good or bad thing. You change everyday and you can't control it even if you want to.

While it might feel nice to say statements like "I'm in control of my life," sometimes things will happen that are completely out of your control. Someone you know may drop dead. You could become extremely rich and famous. A building wall might fall in on you. There could be a global pandemic. You could have everything you care about, or think you care about, taken from you and the only control you have is how you choose to respond to the situation that you've found yourself in. The key to doing this effectively is to look at your circumstances the way they are rather than the way you think you want them to be. Being able to do that allows you to take the most appropriate course of action to deal with your life as it transpires. When you do this objectively you might realise that the things you once saw as problems aren't actually problems. Often it's your interpretation of the scenario that freaks you out more than the scenario itself. Alternatively, you might realise that there are things going on in your life that are a lot worse than you wanted to believe and it's time for you to accept or address them.

MESSAGE RECEIVED

People, businesses, organisations and institutions with a wide range of agendas will feed you information in various forms in an attempt to attract, distract, exploit or influence you. They may have your best interests at heart, they may be actively trying to harm you or they may be indifferent to your existence. It's often impossible to tell and it arguably doesn't matter. The thing that does matter is what you do in response to receiving information, the result of which will have a profound impact on the outcome of your life and mental state. Your responses to information may also impact the lives and mental states of anyone you directly or indirectly interact with.

Sometimes the things you do will be in opposition to wishes of people who you may admire, respect and love. People whose opinions, like yours, can be easily misinformed or driven by personal fear and greed. When you don't do what people want, expect or demand of you then they may go to extreme lengths to try and change your opinion, discredit you, silence you or punish you. They may label you, threaten you, attack you, befriend you, attempt to ruin your credibility or even try to convince you that you've lost your mind. In addition to filtering information skilfully it's, therefore, also important for you to trust yourself to act on the information you receive in a way that is independent of the external pressure of other people.

If you don't understand how information is used in an attempt to control you then you may be highly susceptible to the lure of anyone who can capture your attention and plant ideas in your mind. In doing so they will have you think things, give things, say things, stop doing things or ignore things that could be to your own detriment, to the detriment of other people and even to the detriment of the planet.

POSITIVITY IS POWERFUL

Some people call it manifestation and other people call it optimistic thinking, goal setting, prayer, faith or visualisation. It's all basically the same stuff. The power of positivity is about being able to look beyond your current circumstances to imagine a different future, one which you can look forward to and work productively towards. The power of positivity is knowing that you have the power to turn your circumstances and mindset around, no matter how insurmountable the task seems. It's also knowing that great things can happen to anyone at anytime.

If your situation ever feels hopeless then look for some hope. Imagine what your ideal future looks like and then start doing things to bring that future to life. When you learn how to do this then you'll instantly start to feel better which can also increase your ability to think clearly, dream creatively, take action and produce results.

WARNING 1: It's important that you don't delude yourself about about the situation you're in. In a state of positive delusion you can underestimate the reality of your circumstances which can put you and other people in danger. It can also result in you looking and sounding like a fool.

WARNING 2: Be careful of anyone who tells you that you're not getting what you want in life because you're not being positive enough. The topic of positivity is sometimes used as a form of manipulation that is used in an attempt to get you to do what another person wants.

HOT TIP! If someone guarantees you a result if you follow their formula or thinking positive thoughts then ask them to put that guarantee in writing. If they aren't willing to commit to a guarantee in a formal agreement then they may be offering you empty words. People often make promises that they have no intention or ability to deliver on and the cost of that can be carried by you.

THE TRAP OF PRETENDING

Imagine we are standing at a bar and I ask you who you are. You'll potentially respond with a list of things like "my name is <insert name>, I am <insert age>, I am from <insert country>, I am a <insert job description> and I am <insert sexuality>." All of those things you say about yourself can be true and real, but they are not necessarily you. It's just a list of things you may identify with when all you are is another human being standing at a bar, just like me.

However you shape it, it's highly likely that you'll have an image of yourself and, to you, that image is real. Other people will also have an image of who you are and, to them, that image is real too. Maybe you're a good person, a successful person or a smart person? Maybe you're the dumb one, the wild one, the messy one or the beautiful one? If it's not that then you'll have your own version. The good news is the image you hold in your mind is not you, it's only your view of yourself at a specific moment in time. It might feel real and that's the bad news, because if you believe you're a specific type of person then you're stuck in that role. You're trapped pretending to be a fixed type of human being and that thought separates you from other people who you'll see as different. It will also limit your ability to look at your behaviour and solve problems. For example:

- A person who believes they are independent may not ask for help because, in their mind, they are independent
- A person who believes they are rational may not see when they are being irrational because, in their mind, they are rational
- A person who believes they are tough may not see when they are exposed and weak because, in their mind, they are tough

It's easy to fall into the trap of pretending you are a fixed type of person that is different from other people. Large sums of money are spent studying and categorising people into groups from which they can be separated and influenced into action. Maybe you're not susceptible to this trickery though. Maybe you are a savvy person, unlike those gullible people who are suckers to propaganda or marketing. Or maybe you're one of the enlightened or chosen few, unlike those who aren't. You know those idiots to the left or those idiots to the right? You know the ones.

Sometimes you may feel different, separate or alien to another person, or group of people, and that difference may even be logically justified. Underneath the way you view yourself and present yourself, however, you're just as human as anyone on earth. Just like every human being on earth your thought processes are also easily corruptible and you're capable of expressing all sorts of behaviour - the good, the bad and the ugly. If you're like me then you probably don't want to accept you're capable of expressing certain types of behaviour because then you'd have to confront that you have untapped potential within you. You'd also have to acknowledge that you have the capacity to be vile, given the right circumstances.

Humankind has proven time and time again that everyday people are able to exhibit many types of behaviour, especially when they are put in positions of power or under duress. The Stanford Prison Experiment is arguably the clearest example of this. During the experiment psychologists took twenty-four university students and placed them in a simulated prison environment. They split the group in half and allocated them the role of either a guard or inmate. After only six days the guards became so abusive and the prisoners expressed signs of genuine distress to the point that the experiment was called off. The frightening part is that it only took a small change in the participant's environment, a job title, some clear instructions, a uniform and a little bit of sleep deprivation to trigger these everyday people into a state where they would physically and mentally abuse each other. They embodied the fake roles they had been given. It's useful for you to remember this because whenever you separate yourself from other people then you are at risk of treating those 'others' poorly. When people treat you as separate from them then they are at risk of treating you, the other, poorly as well. The Holocaust, Rwandan genocide and Apartheid are extreme but real world examples of the way this separation can manifest and the consequences are sickening.

Programs of indoctrination will create separation in your mind by conducting ceremonies where you can be fooled into believing you have become something that is different to 'the others'. It's the moment you go from student to graduate, non-citizen to citizen, civilian to soldier or law-abider to criminal. Less obvious versions including being conned into believing that you've fundamentally changed your being - like 'the saved', 'transformed', 'cleansed' or 'personally developed'. Less extreme examples include when you buy a product, consume something or engage in processes of brand activation that leave you feeling part of an exclusive group that is different to other people.

HOT TIP! Lying and pretending are slightly different. When a person lies they know it's a lie because they are intending to deceive you. The trap of pretending is that you can become unintentionally trapped thinking you are a certain type of person that is worth more, less or is fundamentally different from other human beings who are actually just as human as you.

WARNING: When you fall into the trap of thinking someone else is a specific type of person then you'll potentially miss a happy person's cry for help, a stupid person's genius idea, a nasty person's kind offer, a lazy person's effort, a compassionate person's wickedness or an ugly person's beauty.

CHEMICALS ARE CHEEKY

Fear and anxiety are chemical responses activated by your body to threats that could physically harm or kill you (physical threats) and threats that are unlikely to physically harm or kill you (other threats). An example of a physical threat is playing Russian Roulette, a game that is inherently and immediately dangerous to your life regardless of how experienced the player is. An example of an other threat is asking a question in a crowded lecture where the outcome of your actions is unlikely to end your life, but may feel like it nonetheless.

You'll often hear people talking about your body's reaction to threats as 'fight or flight' or an amygdala response. This response is activated by certain chemicals that get you ready to face a threat (fight) or run away from a threat (flight). The combination of chemicals that trigger this response is unnecessary to explain in the context of this chapter. The point is that your body can be flooded with chemicals that cause you to feel a range of emotions, like fear and anxiety, regardless of whether the threat is truly dangerous or not. This means that you can feel equally scared in a situation when there is no physical threat to your safety (like when you're watching a movie in the security of safe home) as you do in a situation when there is an immediate physical threat to your life (like when you're in a fight). In both situations you can feel an equivalent level of fear/anxiety if your survival response is triggered. This is because the chemicals circulating within your body can be the same even though the situations are different. That's why some people can feel just as on edge in a safe environment as they do in a high-risk one. It's also why fearmongering is cruel, even if your cause is worthwhile.

There are lots of people spreading fear in the name of progress, triggering people into a state of terror and then taking no responsibility for the impact they've had on them. It's also why, especially in the era of digital communication, it's useful to have the skills to accurately gauge the reality of the threats you are facing in life. If you ignore a physical threat then it can result in suffering. When you pay too much attention to other threats then you can enter a state of unnecessary fear that also causes suffering.

WHEN FACING THREATS THAT ARE UNLIKELY TO KILL OR HARM (OTHER THREATS)

This is when you want to ask someone out on a date, but you don't do it. It's when you want to tell a joke around friends and you're capable of it, but you don't do it. You stop yourself from taking the plunge and then you justify your reasons for doing so. It could be that you're scared of feeling a certain way, looking a certain way or causing offence to the people around you - all legitimate concerns. Those thoughts can trigger your flight or fight response and you can feel uncomfortable. If you let that uncomfortable feeling overwhelm you then you can freeze. Yet, if you can ignore that feeling and still take action anyway then it's unlikely that anyone will be irreversibly hurt so you may as well go for it. It might feel impossible to start with, but if you tackle these threats head on then you may even get the result you desired. You're also likely to learn something and grow in confidence in the process.

WHEN FACING THREATS THAT COULD KILL OR HARM (PHYSICAL THREATS)

This is the category that extreme sports, epic adventures, rulebreaking and serious risk-taking activities fall into. These are the physically dangerous endeavours that could end your life as you know it, irreversibly damaging you and other people in the process. These are also pursuits that could produce incredible results and provide you with an experience that is genuinely out of this world. People say things like "we're all going to die one day so you may as well go for it." A different way of looking at physical threats is "you only live once so you want to treasure your life and play it safe." There is no right answer or magical ruler to use when working out how much physical risk-taking is appropriate for you in your life. It is worth being aware, however, that you will be required to face some physical threats to live the most basic existence. Anyone who gets into a car, for example, is taking a risk. The reality is that you could die or be horribly injured in a car crash, yet millions of people get into cars everyday without actively questioning whether the risk is worth the reward. Some people will even argue it's necessary which, unless you are physically forced to, it's not. It's a choice. A logical question to ask yourself when facing any physical threat is, therefore, is this risk worth the reward? You'll find the answer always tends to always be yes, only if you come out unscathed. This is the line we all toe and some people are just more aware of it than other people. In the end only you can decide how much physical risk-taking is right for you.

HOT TIP! If you choose to face a threat in the physical category then it makes sense to reduce the threat as much as possible. Then you can really let go and enjoy the experience thoroughly. I'd also encourage you to make sure that you're facing the threat because you honestly want to and not because you're trying to numb yourself, please someone or prove anything to anyone else.

HOT TIP! If you are facing a threat that someone around you knows how to deal with adeptly, and you trust them to look after you, then let them guide you through it. It's a very beautiful thing to detach yourself from your thoughts and let someone competent take the lead. Be careful though! Even if you're following another person's clear orders, advice or instructions, you will ultimately pay the price for your own actions.

WARNING: Everyone's fears look different. It's, therefore, pointless comparing yourself to anyone else. Just because someone can take big risks in any domain of life doesn't mean they're fearless. It could just mean that they're looking for something, that they're running from something, that they're playing in their personal safe zone or that they're naïve to the reality of the threats they are facing.

NOTE: There is a third type of threat that you can call an imagined threat. This is the territory of delusion. It's a belief or altered reality that is persistently held despite evidence or agreement to the contrary. It's why it's advisable to base your decision making around facts. For example, if you went for a swim in the ocean then you could have a great time, you could drown or you could be laughed at by people on the beach for your paddling technique. All those things have happened before and are they are likely to happen again. Swimming in the ocean, therefore, has physical threats and other threats associated with it. An imagined threat, on the other hand, would be that the sun heats up the ocean to the point you are boiled to death. This hasn't happened in recorded in history and it is delusional to think it would happen to you.

FAILURE IS A FALLACY

Learning to deal with your perception of failure is enormously important because things may not always work out the way you want or expect. Regardless of how organised, careful, hardworking and disciplined you are, sometimes life will jump up and slap you. One day you might feel like things are going really well and the next day your life can feel like it's been inexplicably turned on its head. So, how do you deal with perceived failure? That potentially crippling, sickening, paralysing or humiliating feeling when things unexpectedly change or you know that you've really stuffed up? A helpful starting place is to remember that you're not a failure because things haven't worked out the way you wanted, planned for or hoped. You're not in control of everything. Forgive yourself, apologise to anyone you've hurt, learn from your mistakes and move on. That's arguably the most productive way to deal with a perceived failure.

The fallacy of failure goes beyond how to deal with perceived failure and into the understanding that failure doesn't exist other than as a linguistic construct. It's a fallacy in the sense that it only exists in language as an entirely subjective label. That means you can't actually fail, or be a failure, unless you or other people say so. If you understand that fallacy then you'll be able to look at everything that's happened in your life in a completely different way. You can then take a perceived failure and turn it into an opportunity to grow and learn. It's the same thing spun a different way. You will also see that many other barriers in your life simply disappear because they are only created in your mind, through language, and they are not necessarily real.

GAMES AND PLAYERS

You and I could stand together looking at the same view. I could even metaphorically or physically stand in your shoes. I will never, however, be able to experience your exact thoughts, emotions, vision or history. In that sense it's impossible for me to see the world through your eyes in your full experience of life. Your eyes are your eyes only and you're unique. As much as I can seek to understand or share experiences with you, I can only ever be a player (or actor) in your life and you can only ever be a player (or actor) in my life. You could even say we're engaged in a game called life.

From the second we wake up we are playing. Some people play the game of fitness, some people play the game of rule breaking, some people play the game of politics and some people play the game of service. Other people play the game of money accumulation at any cost. The more money they make, the more they win at their game. They'll destroy the environment, ruin cultures and maliciously use other people to hit their targets. Almost everything they do is in line with that game and they are confused when other people don't celebrate their perceived success.

There isn't one game and *the game* is not to be confused with money accumulation, being in positions of power or traditional forms of success. You might never want to be at the top of any field and that's ok. Some people talk about playing *the game* as an excuse for cheating on and lying to other people and they are completely okay with that. They'll also say things that aren't necessarily true in order to justify their behaviour and diminish the impact of their exploits. Conscious players understand that just by living everyone is playing and the same rules don't apply to us all. What is legal in one state or country, for example, may not be legal in another. Unconscious players believe their world view is correct and everyone should follow their rules. That's how naïve travellers who cross the wrong boarder without adjusting their behaviour end up dead or in jail.

It's really useful to know the rules of the games you find yourself playing, otherwise you can get yourself in serious trouble. The challenge you'll find is that some rules are written clearly, like laws, and other rules are more ambiguous, like expectations within a relationship. Sometimes you'll have to write the rules for yourself. If you can identify the games you are playing and clearly define the rules, you'll be able to surround yourself with people who are playing within the same parameters as you. As a result you'll have a better chance of winning and so will they.

CONSIDER THIS: Life is whatever you say it is. Life, therefore, isn't a game unless you say it is. Games, however, are certainly played within life and people are the players who create and play those games.

MATERIAL MADNESS

While there's nothing wrong with working towards nice things, doing fun stuff or trying to fit in with the people around you, you probably want to make sure it doesn't come at the cost of what's really important. By this I mean what's really important *to you*. The *to you* is critical because lots of people will have an opinion about what you should be doing and they'll try to force that opinion on you. That does not mean they necessarily know what the right thing is, *to you*. When you look within yourself then you'll eventually be able to work out what the right thing is. It's potentially the thing you are trying to ignore, justify or put behind the seemingly easy or attractive option. It doesn't have to be the most socially acceptable option either. You don't have keep up with other people's material standards of living. The love of money and material possessions sends some people mad.

HOT TIP! Sometimes the right thing for you to do is to go against the crowd, even if it hurts. Other times the right thing for you to do is go with the crowd, even if it hurts. When you start to do the things you know to do deep down then you'll learn to trust yourself. You may also discover some peace, regardless of the outcome of your actions.

DANGERS OF DRIVE

There are times when being driven can be extremely dangerous, especially if you're someone who will go all out/in and even if you are producing what appears to be successful results. There are lots of ambitious, well-trained and educated people successfully chasing goals while simultaneously causing harm to themselves and other people in the process. That's how some high achieving people end up dying alone, distraught and in pain. They did horrible things and became disconnected from themselves, those they love and those who love them while being driven to get somewhere, get something or be someone. If you don't believe me on that then just ask a palliative care professional.

The danger of drive is understanding that sometimes more action will create more trouble for you, like the gambler who keeps gambling for the win that will solve their financial problems until they bet the family home. While some people produce phenomenal results from being driven, other people are ruined by their drive. If not kept in check then being driven can exhaust you to the point you can't get out of bed. Being driven can expose you to unnecessary danger, it can damage your relationships and it can stop you from being able to absorb good advice from people who are trying to help you. Drive can also blind you from seeing the beauty that is all around you in the world. Being driven also doesn't always mean you're being productive. It doesn't mean you're in the right environment or system. It doesn't guarantee a result and, even if it does produce the result you were focused on, you might miss out on a better opportunity that was staring you in the face while you were desperately chasing something else.

People often confuse drive with performance. They are separate concepts. Being driven does not necessarily make you a high performer. In terms of increased performance there are times when doing nothing is actually a powerful strategy because some things take time to work out or manifest. If you plant a tree today then it will take time to grow. If you invest in your education then you might not see the benefits for years. If you buy shares then they will take time to give you a return and if you get in the way of that process then you will jeopardise the results.

Doing nothing in certain situations is a skill that requires intelligence, focus and patience over the immediate gratification of taking action. This isn't an easy thing to master because to do nothing can sometimes feel like you're failing, are exposed to risk, are missing out or are falling behind other people. That's why this style of thinking is somewhat counterintuitive. In certain situations, however, being able to hold your nerve and pace yourself could save your life. Alcohol, for example, takes a while to kick in and that's why inexperienced drinkers get themselves in trouble by going too hard too fast. Slowing down in certain situations could save your money too. A great sales tool is to put people under intense pressure to take action immediately, not allowing them time to think about what they are actually getting into. Learning how to relax and make good choices regardless of how you feel or what's happening around you can improve your performance in any area of life with a speed that is mind-blowing. That said, it is a gift that you can only give yourself once you learn the beauty of delayed gratification and letting go.

THE NICK OF TIME

Time is a funny thing. On the one hand it's an objective scientific measurement. Each second, minute and hour is the same length as the last. On the other hand our experience of time is radically subjective. You may notice that time seems to slow down when you're doing something boring and speeds up when you're doing something exhilarating, or vice versa. Regardless of how you feel, however, the clock apparently still ticks on the same beat.

As we move through life our minds allow us to remember a version of the past and imagine the future, neither of which is necessarily true. This process is practical, however, because it provides a reference for living that is often referred to as time. The challenge with time is that when we are thinking about the past or dreaming of the future we're not fully aware of what's happening around us in the present moment. We can lose ourselves in thoughts or ideas about the past and future rather than enjoying and influencing what's happening now. That's why thinking is a potentially dangerous artform. It's why your imagination, if not kept in check, can get you into trouble.

You can get so lost in the reality of your thoughts and out of touch with the reality of your physical surroundings and that's how you expose yourself to risk. At the same time, if you don't occasionally stop to think about where you're going or what you're doing then you can become so swept up in the current moment that you forget you have a future on earth that might arrive. A future that will be partly shaped by your actions in the current moment. That's why it's helpful to have a grasp on where you are in time. To do that, you need to intimately appreciate the difference between the past, the present and the future.

KNOWING THE PAST:

The past exists as a memory or a documented history. It has happened and, although you can rewrite it, you can't change what went down. While the past might feel real, it's not. It's in the past. It's done. It's over. If you can accept your past and let it go then you'll be closer to the present moment.

KNOWING THE PRESENT:

The present moment is happening right now. You can only ever do things in the present moment. Even if you're thinking or talking about the past or the future then that thought or communication is happening in the present moment. If you do something now, like buy something online, then your future self will receive the result of your present actions in a new and present moment in the future.

KNOWING THE FUTURE:

Your future on earth might not arrive. It's an imagination or dream because it's not guaranteed and it could turn out completely differently to how you envisage it being. This is one of those concepts that can liberate you or scare you. It can liberate you because it's exciting and can be full of beautiful possibilities. It can scare you because it's unknown and some of those possibilities can be uncomfortable. I hope it liberates you.

REALITY CHECK

A friend recently said to me that "the moment you need help the most is also the moment that you might be least likely to ask for it." I think she's right. Some people are embarrassed by the situation they are in or the things they have thought or done. They may have been hurt by other people who they once trusted and they aren't willing to expose themselves to that pain again. As a result, they close themselves off from everyone as a protection mechanism.

Some people might be working really hard to just get through the day and they could feel like they can't handle another conversation. They might be looking for answers to their troubles outside of their existing social network and, in doing so, they will be isolated from those who genuinely love and care for them. Then there are times when people are screaming out for help and there's no one there to hear their call or their screams are heard by other people who are so absorbed by their own survival that they lack the will or ability to do anything. Then there are people who intentionally and unapologetically prey on the desperation of those looking for support, guidance or a leg up in life. There are entire industries built on exploiting people who are looking for answers to life that don't necessarily exist, unless you blindly believe otherwise. All of these factors, and many more, mean that if someone is looking for help then they might not know where to turn, who to trust or how to ask for it.

I've been in all of the above situations and I know lots of people who have been there too or are currently there now. This includes some of the most adventurous, beautiful and traditionally successful people you could meet. To be clear on this, just because someone looks like they are doing well doesn't mean they are. The opposite of that statement is also true. Just because you think someone isn't doing well doesn't mean they aren't. Sometimes people are intentionally disconnecting from everyone they know in order to think. To stop and think deeply takes a lot of energy and it can leave very little space for anything else. It's also smart because so much of the information that exists in the world is conflicting, commercialised and politicised. A clever way to break free from your social conditioning is, therefore, to find silence and learn to think by yourself. Someone doing that might not look like they are doing well, however, because they're out of the metaphorical rat race. On the flip side, there are highly active members of society who appear to be living perfect existences when, in reality, they are really struggling. They are arguably sick. If you met them, you might never know. Instead you'll only see the superficial stuff that they present to you, splash on social media or drop into a conversation. What they'll show you is a one-sided representation of their existence and some of them will protect that façade like their life depends on it. Some of those people even pay other people to create and manicure a public image for them. As their public image grows they can become so consumed by that image that they forget who they really are, which is just another human being who now has a powerful brand.

The people who are authentic and brave enough to speak openly about the things that are happening in their life can look nuts and unstable. They don't necessarily get rewarded for being real and sometimes they get punished, criticised and shamed. For that reason being truly honest requires a strength that can look like, and is often confused as, weakness. In certain situations, however, being honest is also plain stupid. While it can feel nice to share your thoughts, if you tell the wrong person the wrong thing then it can lead to an unproductive disaster. If some people opened up and shared themselves honestly then they would be ostracised from their communities. Their family would disown them for what they've done, they'd lose their jobs and freedoms. Kids who have grown up in religious settings understand this well so they learn to conform, bend the truth or lie from a young age. Adults working within systems of strict indoctrination also learn this quickly. That's why some people are wary of speaking up, connecting with or sharing their authentic thoughts with you. You are a potential threat to their survival and they may have responsibilities or dreams that, to them, are more important than you are.

It's useful for you to understand this so that when you meet someone you can remind yourself that you aren't necessarily being met with the full reality of their life. If you don't understand this concept then you can be left feeling inadequate in comparison to people who are only presenting the more positive aspects of their behaviour and lifestyle. Worse yet, you might miss the warning signs that someone in your life desperately needs support, some compassion, a firm word or should be cut off. If you don't get this then you won't be open to seeing and hearing the person that's standing in front of you for who they are at a specific moment in time. You won't be able to see beyond their possessions, looks, position of authority, shared history, charisma or language. Instead you'll only see the image of the person that you think you know and that person may not exist anymore. They may be either temporarily or permanently corrupted, or you may have never see them for who they really are in the first place.

THE END

To wake up everyday and find your way through this world can be tough. There are a lot of things that can cause you pain and end your life. Then there are also inescapable realities that you can't run from, like death. When you open your eyes to the reality to all of that then it can take every part of you to break through the anxiety and keep on backing yourself, sharing your love, taking risks, trusting other people and being kind. It can be terrifying, but it's also where the best parts of life seem to happen. Speaking of which, it's taken a huge part of me to write this book and I have lent heavily on a lot of people to bring it to life. To those people, and you know who you are, thank you. A special thank you also goes out to the wonderful Stephanie who lights up my world in different ways everyday.

I have shared this book with you all in an attempt to reach through these pages and let you know that anyone can find themselves in a terrifying situation. If that ever happens to you then please remember these words and hang on. Don't ever give up on yourself, even if it feels unbearable or pointless at the time. Take a breath and try to relax into the chaos. In a split and beautiful second everything can change and there is an unimaginably spectacular side of life that's worth sticking around for... no matter how insurmountable your pain, or hopeless your situation, may seem.

Printed in Australia
AUHW021758070621
346757AU00022B/32/J